the **complete** *series*

Slow Cooker

WILEY

John Wiley & Sons, Inc.

For general information on our other products and services or for technical support, please contact our Customer Care Department within the United States at (800) 762-2974, outside the United States at (317) 572-3993 or fax (317) 572-4002.

Wiley also publishes its books in a variety of electronic formats. Some content that appears in print may not be available in electronic books. For more information about Wiley products, visit our web site at www.wiley.com.

Library of Congress Cataloging-in-Publication Data is available upon request.

978-1-118-11961-7

Printed in China

10 9 8 7 6 5 4 3 2 1

Contents

Introduction

In earlier years, the stockpot was perfect for corned and pickled meats, ideal for soups and casseroles and superb for stewed fruits as it happily bubbled in the hearth during those cold wintry months. However, that was the limit of its usefulness. Now that you are the owner of a new electric version, you will find that there are a great number of dishes that you had never thought could be cooked so well and with so little difficulty.

Having a slow cooker is like having a genie at home, cooking while you are away. When you arrive home, delicious food is waiting and there is no preparation mess to clean up. All of this was done the night before or earlier in the day. Having a slow cooker adds a note of serenity in the kitchen. You are free to relax for a few minutes, and there is even time for a pleasant glass of wine. You do not need to rush, dinner awaits without fear of drying out or overcooking.

Another feature of the slow cooker is that it is also a marvellous food warmer and server. It is excellent for buffets and potlucks. The low temperature setting allows you to keep previously cooked food warm so guests can help themselves. It is ideal for heat-and-serve dishes.

Because the slow cooking concept calls for long cooking, it forces you to organize in advance. It means you get set for dinner early in the day rather than relying on something fast in the evening. You can even perform some of the necessary preparation, such as cutting up the meat, peeling the vegetables and organizing all the other ingredients, the evening before.

Putting the recipe together the next morning takes only a few minutes, when all the prep work is done.

Slow cooking, made possible by low temperature, is the key to fine flavor, juiciness and lack of shrinkage, especially with meat and poultry. Food cooked at low temperature also retains more minerals and vitamins in the food. Low temperature is below 392°F and high is around 572°F.

The wrap-around heating method makes cooking in this way possible. It eliminates all of the heat concentrating on the bottom of the cooker that will generally cause scorching and will require you to spend some time stirring when the food starts to stick.

When the cooker is turned to high, you will find that this temperature is not hot enough to brown the meat. We believe

it is best to brown meat in a frying pan or in the oven prior to placing it into the slow cooker. This will enhance the flavor of your dish. You will get an even better result if you deglaze the frying pan or roasting dish with a little stock or wine then add this to your cooker.

One drawback with slow cooking is the reduction in color of bright colored vegetables, especially peas and beans. A way of keeping the color constant is to only put them into your slow cooker as a last minute inclusion.

All of the recipes in this book are easy to assemble with ingredients that you'll find in your pantry. Once you start experimenting with your slow cooker, you'll know what ingredients to keep on hand for easy meals you can prep the night before, such as dried soup mix, canned stocks, beans and tomatoes. When pot roast or stew meat is on sale, you'll know to stock up so you'll always be able to whip up something homemade

and delicious with very little effort. You might be surprised to learn that slow cookers aren't just for soups and stews— they work for breads and desserts, too.

Our chefs tested and tasted hundreds of recipes and have chosen the best for make ahead meals with the best flavor. Cooking times may vary, depending on the tenderness and texture of the meat, as well as the individual appliance you have, but the times listed in the recipes are a good guideline. Follow the basic instructions in this book and soon you'll find that you'll be able to adapt literally hundreds of your own favorite recipes for slow cooking.

How to clean and care for your slow cooker

- Never submerge the appliance in water. Remove the cooking bowl and place it in the dishwasher or wash with hot soapy water as soon as you empty it. Do not pour in cold water if the bowl is still hot from cooking.

- Do not use abrasive cleaning compounds. A cloth, sponge or rubber spatula will usually remove the residue – if necessary a plastic cleaning pad may be used.

- To remove water spots and other stains, use a non-abrasive cleaner or vinegar, and wipe with olive oil to restore the sparkle.

- The metal liner may be cleaned with a damp cloth or scouring pad, or sprayed lightly with all-purpose cleaner to maintain its original sheen.

- The outside of the appliance may be cleaned with a soft cloth and warm soapy water and wiped dry. Do not use abrasive cleaners on the outside.

- Care should be taken in not bumping the ceramic insert with metal spoons or water taps. A sharp knock can break or chip the bowl.

- Do not put frozen or very cold foods in the slow cooker if the appliance has been pre-heated or is hot to the touch.

Safety hints

When using electrical appliances, basic safety precautions should always be followed, including the following:

- Read all instructions and become thoroughly familiar with the unit.

- Do not touch hot surfaces – always use handles or knobs.

- To protect against electrical hazards, do not immerse cord, plugs or cooking unit in water or other liquid.

- Close supervision is necessary when appliance is in use or near children.

- Unplug from outlet when not in use, before putting on or taking off parts, and before cleaning.

- Do not operate an appliance with a damaged cord or plug or after the appliance malfunctions or has been damaged in any manner. Return appliance to nearest authorized service facility for examination, repair or adjustment.

- The use of accessory attachments not recommended by the manufacturer may cause a hazard.

- Do not use outdoors or on a wet surface.

- Do not let the cord hang over the edge of the counter or table, or touch hot surfaces.

- Do not place slow cooker units on or near a hot gas or electric burner, or in a heated oven.

- Extreme caution must be used when moving the appliance containing hot oil or other liquids.

- Always attach to appliance first, then plug cord into the wall outlet. To disconnect, turn any control to off, then remove the plug from the wall outlet.

- Do not use the appliance for other than its intended use.

Satisfying Soups

Y ou can extend the pleasures of the winter soup pot to all months of the year. A light, clear soup provides a delicious prelude to a more substantial meal, regardless of the season. Often summer-jaded palates appreciate the delicacy of a consommé or chilled soup and the slow cooker provides these without hours of slaving over a hot stove. For those hearty soups, try starting your soup on a Friday night and gently cooking it through the night to serve when the team arrives for Saturday lunch.

Consommé

2 lb/1kg lean beef on the bone, such as chuck roast
1 leek, roughly chopped
1 large onion, roughly chopped
2 bay leaves
1 clove garlic, chopped
1 stalk celery with leaves, roughly chopped
3 whole sprigs of parsley, plus ¼ cup, chopped
salt and freshly ground black pepper
¼ cup dry sherry

1 Place all ingredients except parsley and sherry in slow cooker and add 12 cups of water. Simmer on low for 8 hours or longer. Remove cooking bowl from slow cooker and let cool completely.

2 Carefully remove all the fat and take out all large pieces of meat and vegetables, then strain the consommé through cheesecloth or a fine strainer. Serve piping hot with 2 teaspoons of dry sherry in each bowl and a sprinkle of freshly chopped parsley to garnish.

Serves 6 • Preparation 20 minutes • Cooking 8 hours

Savory Butternut Squash Soup

1 kg/2 lb butternut squash, peeled, diced
400mL/14 oz tomato juice
1 tablespoon raw sugar
salt and freshly ground black pepper
1 bay leaf
3 drops of Tabasco sauce
2 chicken bouillon cubes
½ cup heavy cream
2 tablespoons chopped fresh Italian parsley

1 Combine all ingredients except cream and parsley with 8 cups water in a slow cooker and cook for 6½ hours on low.

2 Remove bay leaf. Process the mixture a cupful at a time in a food processor.

3 Return mixture to slow cooker and reheat for 15 minutes. Add cream and allow to warm through.

4 Serve sprinkled with fresh parsley.

Serves 6 • Preparation 15 minutes • Cooking 6 hours 45 minutes

Tomato, Lentil and Basil Soup

½ cup lentils (brown or green)
2 lb/1kg Roma or plum tomatoes
2 onions, diced
2 tablespoons sun-dried tomato paste
3 cups vegetable stock
1 bay leaf
freshly ground black pepper
½ cup fresh basil, chopped

1 Rinse the lentils, drain and add them to a large saucepan of boiling water. Simmer, covered, for 25 minutes or until tender, then drain, rinse and set aside.

2 Meanwhile, place the tomatoes in a bowl, cover with boiling water and leave for 30 seconds, then drain. Remove the skins, remove seeds and chop.

3 In a slow cooker on high, add the onions and stir in the tomatoes, tomato paste, stock, bay leaf and pepper. Cover and simmer for 2¼ hours.

4 Remove and discard the bay leaf, then purée the soup until smooth in a food processor or with a hand-held blender. Stir in the lentils and chopped basil, then reheat on high. Serve garnished with fresh basil.

Serves 4 • Preparation 40 minutes • Cooking 3 hours

Roasted Tomato, Red Pepper and Bread Soup

2 tablespoons olive oil
2 lb/1kg Roma or plum tomatoes
2 red peppers
3 cloves garlic, crushed
2 onions, finely diced
2 teaspoons ground cumin
1 teaspoon ground coriander
4 cups chicken stock
2 slices white bread, crusts removed and torn into pieces
1 tablespoon balsamic vinegar
salt and freshly ground black pepper

1 Preheat oven to 350°F/180°C. On a cookie sheet, drizzle tomatoes and peppers
   with olive oil and toss to coat. Roast for 20 minutes or until the skins have
   blistered. Add garlic, onion, cumin and coriander for five additional minutes.
   Let cool. Remove the skins from the tomatoes and peppers and roughly chop.
2 Set slow cooker on high, add the cooked vegetables and stock and cook for
   2 hours. Add bread, balsamic vinegar and salt and pepper, and cook for an
   additional 50 minutes.

Serves 4 • Preparation 30 minutes • Cooking 2 hours 30 minutes

Ham and Split Pea Soup

1½ cups dried split peas
1 onion, diced
2 bay leaves
1 sprig thyme
salt and freshly ground black pepper
1 medium smoked ham hock
8 cups chicken or vegetable stock

1 Rinse peas and place in slow cooker. Add all remaining ingredients to slow cooker and cook on low for at least 8 hours. This soup improves with long, slow cooking, so 10–12 hours will enhance the flavor.
2 Remove bay leaves, thyme and ham hock. Discard the fat from the ham hock, chop the meat and add it to the soup. Serve very hot.

Serves 6–8 • Preparation 20 minutes • Cooking 8–12 hours

Porcini Mushroom Soup

15g/½ oz dried porcini mushrooms
2 tablespoons olive oil
2 cloves garlic, crushed
1 leek, sliced
6 shallots, chopped
10 oz/300g white or button mushrooms, thinly sliced
1 lb/500g wild mushrooms, such as shiitake, cremini, or portabellas, thinly sliced

2 tablespoons all-purpose flour
4 cups chicken, beef or vegetable stock
1 cup heavy cream
½ bunch fresh flat-leaf parsley, chopped
30 fresh basil leaves, shredded
1 tablespoon fresh oregano
salt and freshly ground black pepper
ground nutmeg

1 Add the dried porcinis to ½ cup boiling water. When the mushrooms have softened, remove them from the liquid and set aside. Strain the mushroom liquid through a coffee-filter lined strainer to remove any sand and grit, and reserve the liquid.

2 Heat the olive oil in a large saucepan and add the garlic, leek and shallots and cook until golden (about 3 minutes). Add all the fresh mushrooms and cook over a very high heat until they soften and their liquid evaporates (about 7 minutes). Reserve a few mushroom pieces for the garnish.

3 Transfer the leek and mushroom mixture to a slow cooker preheated on high, then sprinkle with the flour and stir well to enable the flour to be absorbed. Add the stock and the porcini, together with the reserved liquid. Stir to combine and cook for 2 hours.

4 Add the cream, then turn cooker to low and cook for a further 30 minutes or until slightly thickened. Add half the parsley and the basil and oregano and season to taste with salt and pepper. Serve sprinkled with remaining parsley, reserved mushrooms and a sprinkling of ground nutmeg.

Serves 6 • Preparation 40 minutes • Cooking 3 hours

Scallop Chowder

12 sea scallops, quartered
½ cup white wine
1 sprig thyme
1 bay leaf
1 cup heavy cream
12 cups milk
2 cups chicken stock
salt and freshly ground black pepper
6 green onions, chopped

1 Place scallops into slow cooker with white wine and herbs and cook on low for 1 hour.
2 Combine remaining ingredients and add to slow cooker. Cook on high for 1–1½ hours or on low for 1½–2 hours until heated through, but do not overcook.

Serves 4–6 • Preparation 10 minutes • Cooking 2–3 hours

German Potato Soup

1 bunch scallions
2 tablespoons olive oil
1 medium cauliflower, cut into florets (reserve small florets)
600g/1¼ lb potatoes, peeled, diced
1 teaspoon caraway seeds, plus extra for garnish
6 cups vegetable stock
2 tablespoons plain yogurt

1 Cut 2 in/5cm lengths off the end of each scallion. Using a sharp knife, slice these into thin strips, keeping one end intact to hold the strips together. Plunge the strips into a bowl of iced water and set aside until they curl (about 1 hour). Slice the remaining scallions.
2 Heat the olive oil in a slow cooker on a high setting and add the remaining scallion and the cauliflower florets, potatoes and caraway seeds and cook for 50 minutes.
3 Add the stock and bring the soup to the simmer for 2 hours, then process with a food processor or hand-held blender until smooth. Add the reserved small cauliflower florets and simmer for 45 minutes. Serve the soup with a dollop of yogurt, a sprinkling of caraway seeds and the scallion curls.

Serves 6 • Preparation 20 minutes • Cooking 3 hours 35 minutes

Bouillabaisse

3 kg/6 lb mixed fish and seafood, including firm white fish fillets, shrimp, mussels, crab and calamari
¼ cup olive oil
2 cloves garlic, crushed
2 large onions, chopped
2 leeks, sliced
800g/28 oz canned tomatoes
⅔ cup fish stock
1 teaspoon dried thyme
1½ teaspoons dried basil
2 tablespoons chopped fresh parsley
2 bay leaves
2 tablespoons finely grated orange zest
1 teaspoon saffron threads
⅔ cup dry white wine
freshly ground black pepper

1 Remove the bones and skin from the fish fillets and cut into 1 in/2cm cubes. Peel and devein the shrimp, leaving the tails intact. Scrub and remove the beards from the mussels. Cut the crab into quarters. Set aside.

2 Heat a slow cooker on a high setting, then add the oil, garlic, onions, leeks, tomatoes and stock and cook for 1½ hours. Add the thyme, basil, parsley, bay leaves, orange zest, saffron and wine. Cook for 30 minutes.

3 Add the fish and crab and cook for 1 hour. Add the remaining seafood and cook for 1 hour longer or until all fish and seafood are cooked. Season to taste with black pepper.

Serves 6 • Preparation 40 minutes • Cooking 4 hours

Savory Beef, Pork and Lamb

Those of us who are fully aware of the advantages of a slow cooker find cooking and entertaining much simpler. You can prep your main course the night before and pop everything into the slow cooker in the morning and forget about it. Your dinner will cook itself, while you're free to enjoy your family and friends without being tied to the stove. The best part—slow cooker dinners mean quick and easy clean up, too!

Hearty Beef Stew

1 tablespoon vegetable oil
2 lb/1kg pot roast or chuck roast, trimmed and cubed
2 onions, chopped
2 beef bouillon cubes, crumbled
2 carrots, sliced
1 parsnip, sliced
salt and freshly ground black pepper
1 bouquet garni*
1 oz/30g butter, room temperature
2 tablespoons all-purpose flour

1 Pat meat cubes dry with paper towel and season with salt and pepper. Heat oil in a large skillet and brown meat on all sides, being careful not to crowd the pan, or the beef will steam, not brown. Remove meat to a plate and continue to brown meat in batches if necessary.

2 Mix bouillon cubes in 1 cup of hot water, stirring to dissolve.

3 Place stock, meat, onion, carrots, parsnip, salt and pepper and bouquet garni in slow cooker. Cook for approximately 7–8 hours on low or 6–7 hours on high. Remove bouquet garni. Stir butter and flour together and stir into the stew. Serve with rice or pasta and garnish with chopped fresh parsley.

*Bouquet garni is a collection of herbs, traditionally fresh parsley, fresh or dried thyme, and bay leaf that are tied together in a bundle so they can be removed easily at the end of the cooking.

Serves 4–5 • Preparation 25 minutes • Cooking 6–8 hours

Ginger Beef

3 onions, finely chopped
1 clove garlic, crushed
1½ in/4cm piece ginger, finely chopped
2 teaspoons salt
½ teaspoon hot sauce, such as Tabasco
3 lb/1½ kg pot roast or chuck roast, cubed
1(14 ounce) can diced tomatoes, drained
1 cup beef stock

1 Place onion, garlic, ginger, salt and hot sauce in a food processor or blender and blend to a purée.

2 Mix meat and purée and allow to stand for at least 3 hours, turning meat occasionally.

3 Place meat in slow cooker and add tomatoes and beef stock. Cook on high for 1 hour, then on low for 4 hours or until meat is tender. Serve with rice, garnished with lemon quarters.

Serves 6 • Preparation 3 hours 25 minutes • Cooking 5 hours

Beef and Chickpea Stew

2 tablespoons oil
2 lb/1kg lean stew beef, trimmed and cubed
2 onions, sliced
2 cloves garlic, chopped
1 eggplant, diced
1 cup beef stock
14 oz/400g canned whole peeled tomatoes, chopped
¼ cup quick cooking tapioca
1 teaspoon ground cinnamon
1 bay leaf
2 teaspoons salt
freshly ground black pepper
14 oz/400g canned chickpeas or garbanzo beans, rinsed and drained

1 Pat beef cubes dry with paper towel and season beef with salt and pepper. Heat oil in a large skillet and brown meat on all sides, being careful not to crowd the pan, or beef will steam, not brown. Remove meat to a plate and continue to brown meat in batches if necessary. Add all of the browned beef to the pan, plus the eggplant, onions and garlic and cook for 5 minutes, stirring constantly. Drain off excess fat and pour mixture into the slow cooker.

2 Combine stock with juice from canned tomatoes, tapioca, cinnamon, bay leaf, salt and pepper and pour into slow cooker, stirring well. Cover and cook on low for 8 hours.

3 Approximately 30 minutes before serving, turn to high. Stir in chickpeas and tomatoes and cook for the remaining time. Serve garnished with oregano leaves.

Serves 6 • Preparation 30 minutes • Cooking 8 hours

Mexican-Style Beef

4 thin-cut beef sirloin steaks
4 strips bacon, finely chopped
1 tablespoon chopped fresh parsley
½ teaspoon dried marjoram
1 cup fresh breadcrumbs
½ cup all-purpose flour
salt and freshly ground black pepper
toothpicks
1 tablespoon olive oil
1 teaspoon chili powder
1 onion, diced
2 cloves garlic, crushed
1 red bell pepper, diced
1 cup beef stock
2 cups canned red kidney beans, rinsed, drained

1 Place each steak between two pieces of plastic wrap and pound until ¼ in thick. Set aside. Heat a large skillet over medium heat. Add bacon and cook for 3 minutes, draining off any excess fat. Remove from the heat and mix with the parsley, marjoram and breadcrumbs.

2 Combine the flour, salt and pepper in a shallow dish. Divide the bacon mixture between slices of the beef, then roll up each slice from the short end, dredge it in the seasoned flour and secure it with a tooth pick.

3 Heat the oil in a large skillet over medium heat, add the beef and cook for 2 minutes, turning, until browned. Remove from skillet and place in a slow cooker set on low. Add the chili powder, onion, garlic and bell pepper. Gently pour over the stock. Cover the dish then cook for 6 hours. Add the kidney beans and cook for another 3 hours. Remove the cocktail sticks to serve.

Serves 4 • Preparation 20 minutes • Cooking 9 hours 10 minutes

Stuffed Pot Roast

2 lb/1kg top round roast
salt and freshly ground black pepper
½ cup soft breadcrumbs
1(28 ounce) can whole tomatoes
2 canned anchovies, finely mashed (optional)
½ clove garlic, crushed
¼ cup parsley, chopped
1 teaspoon dried basil
2 red peppers, chopped
1 small onion, chopped
2 onions, sliced
1 tablespoon olive oil
1–2 tablespoons all-purpose flour

1 Pat beef dry with paper towel. With a sharp knife, carefully cut a deep slit into the side of the roast that you will be able to fill with stuffing.

2 Chop two of the canned tomatoes, and mix with breadcrumbs, anchovies, garlic, parsley and half of the basil, half of the peppers, and the chopped onion. Season with salt and pepper. Carefully stuff mixture into the opening of the beef and tie with string to keep in place. Season with salt and pepper.

3 Heat oil in large skillet and brown meat on both sides, then place in slow cooker. Add the rest of the canned tomatoes, the sliced onions, remaining basil, red pepper. Cook on high setting for about 4 hours or on low setting for 6–7 hours.

4 To serve, remove meat from liquid and keep warm, then whisk just enough flour into gravy to thicken it. Slice meat and serve with gravy.

Serves 4–6 • Preparation 25 minutes • Cooking 4–7 hours

Beef Braised in Red Wine

½ cup olive oil
700g/1½ lb beef stew meat, trimmed of fat, cut into 2½ in (6cm) chunks
6 shallots, finely chopped
2 cloves garlic, crushed
2 stalks celery, sliced
200g/7 oz button mushrooms, sliced
½ teaspoon ground allspice
1½ cups full-bodied red wine
1 cup tomato purée
2 sprigs fresh thyme
salt and freshly ground black pepper

1 Heat the oil in a large saucepan and cook the meat over high heat, stirring, for
   5 minutes until browned. Remove from pan, then add the shallots, garlic and celery.
   Cook, stirring, for 4 minutes until browned. Add the mushrooms and cook for 1 minute
   or until softened.

2 In a slow cooker set on high add the allspice, wine and tomato purée, then all of the
   fried ingredients. Add 1 sprig of thyme and the seasoning. Cover and cook for 4 hours.

3 Season with salt and pepper, garnish with thyme and serve with mashed potatoes.

Serves 4 • Preparation 20 minutes • Cooking 4 hours 10 minutes

Beef with Olives

2 tablespoons vegetable oil
2 lb/1kg stew beef, cubed
1 tablespoon brandy
1 cup red wine
salt and freshly ground black pepper
1 bouquet garni*
½ clove garlic, crushed
rind of ½ orange
4 oz/120g small black olives
8 sprigs fresh thyme, leaves removed and stalks discarded

1 In a heavy-based frying pan, heat the oil and brown meat.

2 In a small saucepan, heat the brandy and set it alight. Pour over meat in frying pan and allow to burn out.

3 Transfer meat and juices to the slow cooker and add red wine, salt and pepper, bouquet garni, garlic and orange rind. Cook on low for at least 5 hours or overnight.

4 Add the olives for approximately the last hour of cooking. If the sauce is too thin, remove the meat from the slow cooker, set to high and cook until reduced. Alternatively, drain off sauce and reduce it in a saucepan on the stovetop. To serve, remove the orange rind and bouquet garni and sprinkle with thyme.

*Bouquet garni is a collection of herbs, traditionally fresh parsley, fresh or dried thyme, and bay leaf that are tied together in a bundle so they can be removed easily at the end of the cooking.

Serves 6–8 • Preparation 30 minutes • Cooking 5–8 hours

Pot Roast with Red Wine

4 lb/2kg boneless beef chuck roast or pot
roast, trimmed of fat
2 cloves garlic, finely sliced, plus 1 clove
crushed
1 tablespoon vegetable oil
1 large onion, sliced
3 tablespoons brandy
½ cup red wine
6 slices cooked bacon, roughly chopped
3 carrots, roughly chopped

2 bay leaves
3 sprigs fresh parsley
3 sprigs fresh thyme
salt and freshly ground black pepper
1 cup beef stock or water, warmed

1 Pat beef cubes dry with paper towel. Carefully insert the tip of a sharp knife into the
   meat, one inch apart, and push garlic slices into the cuts.

2 Season beef with salt and pepper. Heat oil in a large skillet and brown meat on all
   sides, remove to a plate. Add onions and stir to loosen the brown bits from the bottom
   of the pan. Reduce heat and saute until onions are soft and golden.

3 Add the brandy, stand back and ignite with a match to burn off the alcohol. Put the
   meat back in the pan, add wine and let simmer for approximately 5 minutes. Transfer
   mixture to slow cooker.

4 Add bacon, carrots, crushed garlic, herbs to slow cooker, warm stock or water to
   slow cooker. Season with salt and pepper and cook on low setting for approximately
   6 hours, testing for tenderness after 5 hours. Meat must not be cooked to the point
   where it falls apart. Remove meat and let rest.

5 Strain sauce and let cool until fat rises to the top of the mixture. Skim off the fat and
   strain again. Reduce liquid until it has thickened slightly. Slice beef and serve with
   sauce and steamed vegetables.

Serves 6–8 • Preparation 45 minutes • Cooking 6–7 hours

Braised Beef and Onions

1½ lb/750g round steak, cut into four pieces
2 tablespoons all-purpose flour
2 oz/60g butter
1 large Spanish or yellow onion, peeled and sliced
salt and freshly ground black pepper
1 cup beef stock
1 teaspoon Angostura bitters (optional)

1　Season beef with salt and pepper. Dredge beef in flour to coat.
2　Heat butter in a large skillet on medium high heat. Brown steaks on both sides and place in slow cooker. Add sliced onion to pan and sauté until golden brown.
3　Add onion to slow cooker with salt and pepper, stock and bitters, if using. Cook on low for 6–8 hours.

Serves 4–5 • Preparation 30 minutes • Cooking 6–8 hours

Braised Short Ribs

2 tablespoons all-purpose flour
1 tablespoon sweet paprika
salt and freshly ground black pepper
1½ lb/750g short beef ribs
1 tablespoon vegetable oil
3 onions, sliced
1 carrot, sliced
2 tablespoons beef stock
1 canned crushed tomatoes
1 teaspoon sugar (optional)

1 Mix together flour, paprika, salt and pepper. Pat beef ribs dry with paper towel and rub with spice mixture.

2 Heat the oil in a large skillet. Brown ribs on all sides and transfer to slow cooker.

3 Add a little more oil to frying pan, if necessary, and sauté onion until golden brown. Pour contents of pan into slow cooker, add the carrot and stock and stir.

4 Mix tomatoes into meat mixture. Cook for 6–8 hours on low setting or 5–6 hours on high setting. Season to taste. If too acidic, add 1 teaspoon of sugar. Allow dish to cool, skim off fat and reheat to serve.

Serves 4 • Preparation 30 minutes • Cooking 5–8 hours

Chili Tacos

2 teaspoons vegetable oil
500g/1 lb ground beef
2 onions, chopped
60g/2 oz taco seasoning mix
½ teaspoon freshly ground black pepper
2 tablespoons tomato paste
½ cup beef stock
6 taco shells or corn tortillas

1 Heat the oil in a large skillet, and brown beef. Add onion and cook until slightly
   softened. Stir in taco mix, pepper and tomato paste and cook for 1–2 minutes.
   Add stock and stir.
2 Transfer mixture to slow cooker and cook for approximately 4 hours on low.
   If mixture is too wet at the end of the cooking time, remove the cooker lid and
   cook on high until liquid has reduced.
3 Spoon beef mixture into heated taco shells or tortillas and serve at once with
   bowls of chopped tomatoes, cucumber and lettuce.

Serves 6 • Preparation 25 minutes • Cooking 4–5 hours

Spaghetti and Meatballs

1 lb/500g ground beef
2 white onions, finely chopped
1 clove garlic, crushed
1 tablespoon vegetable oil
½ teaspoon dried basil
1 bay leaf
salt and freshly ground black pepper
14 oz/400g canned tomatoes, drained
2 teaspoons Worcestershire sauce
3 tablespoons tomato paste
1 lb/500g whole grain or whole wheat spaghetti
1 oz/30g Parmesan cheese, grated

1 Mix together meat, onion and garlic, and roll into small balls. Heat the oil in a frying pan, add the meatballs and sauté until lightly browned.

2 Place meatballs into slow cooker and add all remaining ingredients, except pasta and cheese. Cook on low for approximately 4 hours.

3 Bring a large saucepan of salted water to a boil, add the spaghetti and cook for 8 minutes or until just firm in the center (al dente). Drain, then add to slow cooker and stir through sauce. Serve sprinkled with Parmesan cheese.

Serves 4 • Preparation 25 minutes • Cooking 4 hours

Beef Pot Pie

2 tablespoons vegetable oil
2 lb/1kg round steak or chuck roast, cubed
1 onion, chopped
2 tablespoons all-purpose flour
2 beef bouillon cubes, crumbled
1 tablespoon tomato paste
½ teaspoon salt
¼ cup fresh parsley, chopped
1 teaspoon Worcestershire sauce
hot sauce, such as Tabasco
8 oz/250g pre-made puff pastry
2 tablespoons milk

1 Heat oil in a large skillet. Season beef with salt and pepper. Brown beef and onions and transfer to slow cooker using a slotted spoon. Stir flour into pan juices and cook, stirring for 1–2 minutes until slightly browned. Add 1 cup water, bouillon, tomato paste, and salt. Bring to a boil, stirring occasionally.

2 Pour liquid into slow cooker with the parsley, Worcestershire sauce and Tabasco to taste, and cook on low for at least 6–8 hours or overnight. Test meat for tenderness, then spoon beef mixture into a greased 10-inch pie plate or 6 individual oven-safe bowls. Allow to cool.

3 Preheat oven to 375°F/190°C. Slice puff pastry into long strips. Brush rim pie plate or individual bowls with a little milk and fit a pastry strip around the wet rim. Use remaining strips to create a lattice across the meat. Brush with milk and bake individual pies for 20 minutes and large pie for 25–30 minutes.

Recipe makes one whole pie or 6 individual pies.

Serves 6 • Preparation 35 minutes • Cooking 7–9 hours

French Onion Stew

1½ kg/3 lb beef stew meat, trimmed, cut into large cubes
2 tablespoons quick-cooking tapioca
1¾ cup beef stock
100g/3½ oz mushrooms, sliced
4 tablespoons butter
6 medium onions, thinly sliced
pinch salt
¼ cup heavy cream
fresh thyme leaves to garnish

1 Combine beef, tapioca, stock and mushrooms in a slow cooker, cover and cook on high for 4 hours.
2 Meanwhile, melt butter in a large heavy-based skillet over low heat. Add onion and cook, stirring, for 45 minutes or until caramelized and dark brown in color. Add the caramelized onions to the slow cooker and stir to combine. Continue to cook all ingredients together for remaining time.
3 Just before serving stir through cream. Serve the stew on a bed of rice, garnished with fresh thyme.

Serves 6 • Preparation 20 minutes • Cooking 7 hours

Vitello Tonnato

1½ lb/750g veal roast from leg or loin
1 cup white wine or dry cider
1 teaspoon salt
10 peppercorns
1 bay leaf
1 clove garlic
1 teaspoon dried tarragon
1 large white onion, sliced
2 teaspoons white vinegar

Sauce
3 oz/90g canned tuna in water, drained
juice and zest of ½ lemon
½ cup coleslaw dressing
1 egg yolk
1 teaspoon seasoned pepper blend

1 Pour 1¼ cups water into slow cooker. Add veal, wine or cider, salt, peppercorns, bay leaf, garlic, tarragon, onion and vinegar. Cook on low for approximately 4 hours or on high for approximately 2½–3 hours. Check for tenderness, as times will vary depending on quality of meat – do not overcook. Allow meat to cool fully, then remove from stock and slice thinly. Reserve around 2 tablespoons of the stock.

2 To make the sauce, add the tuna, lemon juice and a tablespoon of coleslaw dressing to a food processor or blender and purée.

3 Beat the egg yolk into remaining coleslaw dressing and mix in the tuna purée, pepper blend and grated lemon zest. Add reserved veal stock and blend well – the mixture should have the consistency of half and half.

4 To serve, arrange veal in overlapping slices on a platter, then spoon over the sauce. Serve with salad.

Serves 6 • Preparation 40 minutes • Cooking 3 hours

Beef Stew with Dumplings

450g/1 lb beef stew meat, trimmed of fat, cut into 1 in (25mm) cubes
2 carrots, diced
2 leeks, sliced
1 onion, diced
1 cup beef stock
salt and freshly ground black pepper
400g/14 oz canned butter beans, rinsed, drained
4 tablespoons frozen peas

Cheese Dumplings
⅔ cup self-rising flour
½ teaspoon baking powder
1 teaspoon finely chopped fresh Italian parsley
60g/2 oz Cheddar cheese, grated
60g/2 oz butter, cut into small cubes
2 tablespoons water

1 Place the meat and the vegetables in a slow cooker set on a high setting. Stir in the stock and season well. Cover and cook for 3½ hours.

2 Meanwhile, make the dumplings by combining all the dry ingredients in a bowl. Using your fingertips, rub in the butter and water to form a soft dough.

3 Preheat the oven to 360°F/180°C.

4 Shape the dough into 12 equal dumplings. Stir the butter beans and peas into the casserole, taste and adjust the seasoning.

5 Arrange the dumplings over the top and put the uncovered dish in the oven for 30 minutes or until the dumplings are golden.

This recipe requires you to finish the dumplings in the oven so you will need to use a slow cooker with a cooking dish that can be removed from the electrical component and safely put into the oven.

Serves 4 • Preparation 25 minutes • Cooking 4 hours

Roast Lamb with Root Vegetables

2 tablespoons olive oil
2 parsnips, cut into large chunks
1 medium sweet potato, cut into large chunks
6 cippolini onions
2 cloves garlic, crushed
4 lamb shanks
¾ cup beef stock
¼ cup water
½ cup dry red wine
1 tablespoon tomato paste
1 sprig rosemary
1 bouquet garni*
salt and freshly ground black pepper

1 Heat 1 tablespoon of the oil in a large heavy-based saucepan, add the vegetables and cook until brown. Set aside on a plate. Add the extra oil to the pan and brown the garlic and lamb for a few minutes.

2 Transfer the lamb and garlic to a slow cooker set on high and add the stock, water, red wine, tomato paste, rosemary, bouquet garni, pepper and salt. Cook for 30 minutes, then reduce the heat to low and cook for an additional 7 hours.

3 Add the vegetables to the slow cooker and continue to cook for another hour, until everything is cooked. Before serving, remove the bouquet garni and check the seasoning.

*Bouquet garni is a collection of herbs, traditionally fresh parsley, fresh or dried thyme, and bay leaf that are tied together in a bundle so they can be removed easily at the end of the cooking.

Serves 4 • Preparation 20 minutes • Cooking 8 hours 40 minutes

Swedish Meatballs

1½ cups white breadcrumbs
1 cup buttermilk
500g/1 lb ground pork
250g/½ lb ground beef
2 eggs
1 medium onion, finely chopped
2 teaspoons salt
¾ teaspoon dill seeds
¼ teaspoon allspice
⅛ teaspoon ground nutmeg
4 tablespoons butter
1 cup chicken stock
½ cup dry white wine
freshly ground black pepper
1 cup cream
2 tablespoons fresh parsley leaves to garnish

1 Soak breadcrumbs in buttermilk for 5 minutes. Add meats, eggs, onion, salt, herbs and spices. Mix well, cover and refrigerate for 30 minutes.
2 Shape tablespoon quantities of mixture into balls.
3 Heat butter in a medium skillet and cook meatballs until lightly browned.
4 Place meatballs into the slow cooker as they are browned. Add stock, wine and pepper. Cover and cook on low for 5 hours.
5 Approximately 20 minutes before serving turn the heat to high and add cream. Serve meatballs garnished with parsley and accompanied by crusty bread.

The meatballs will have a finer texture if the meats are ground together twice (ask your butcher to do this).

Serves 6 • Preparation 1 hour 45 minutes • Cooking 5 hours 20 minutes

Roast Pork with Apples

1½ kg/3 lb pork loin, tied with kitchen string
salt and freshly ground black pepper
3 Granny Smith apples, peeled, cored, quartered
1 tablespoon brown sugar
2 teaspoons ground ginger
1 teaspoon salt
1 tablespoon cornstarch
1 tablespoon water

1 Rub pork with salt and pepper. Arrange apples in base of slow cooker. Place pork on top of apples.
2 Combine brown sugar, ginger and salt. Spoon over top surface of pork. Cover and cook on low for 7 hours.
3 Ten minutes before serving strain off 1 cup of liquid into a small saucepan. Blend cornstarch with water to make a smooth paste and stir into liquid. Heat until thickened. Remove string from the pork and carve. Serve with sauce, accompanied by the apples and freshly steamed vegetables.

Serves 6 • Preparation 15 minutes • Cooking 7 hours

Indonesian Spare Ribs

750g/3 lb pork spare ribs
1½ tablespoons peanut oil
1 teaspoon ground coriander
½ teaspoon ground cumin
½ teaspoon freshly ground black pepper
2 tablespoons soy sauce
1 tablespoon tamarind concentrate
1 teaspoon brown sugar
¼ cup water

Paste
2 shallots, chopped
2 cloves garlic
2 teaspoons finely grated fresh ginger
¼ cup water

1 Pound the paste ingredients in a mortar and pestle or combine in a small
   food processor.
2 Chop spare ribs in half. Heat 1 tablespoon of oil in a wok or medium skillet.
   Add spare ribs in 2 batches and fry for 2–3 minutes or until ribs are golden
   and crisp. Remove and set aside.
3 Heat remaining oil and add paste. Cook for 2 minutes, stirring constantly.
   Add coriander, cumin, black pepper, soy sauce, tamarind and sugar.
4 Add the ribs and sauce to the slow cooker, set on high. Add water and cook
   for 4 hours, basting and turning every hour. Add a little extra water if sauce
   becomes too thick. Serve with Chinese greens and a side bowl of rice.

Serves 4 • Preparation 10 minutes • Cooking 4 hours 10 minutes

Pork and Beans

250g/8 oz white or cannellini beans, soaked overnight, drained
2 tablespoons olive oil
500g/1 lb bacon or ham hock, diced
1 large onion, chopped
1 clove garlic, crushed
400g/14 oz canned diced tomatoes
1 bay leaf
2 sprigs fresh thyme
1 sprig fresh marjoram
2 tablespoons dark brown sugar
1 tablespoon corn syrup
1 tablespoon tomato paste
2 teaspoons Angostura bitters
3 teaspoons Dijon mustard
salt and freshly ground black pepper
¼ cup tomato juice

1 Heat the oil in a large skillet over medium heat. Add meat and cook until browned. Remove meat from skillet. Cook onion for 3 minutes. Add garlic and cook for an additional 2 minutes.

2 Layer beans, onions and tomatoes in a slow cooker. Top with meat and add the herbs (tied into a bouquet with kitchen string).

3 Mix together sugar, corn syrup, tomato paste, bitters, mustard, salt, pepper and tomato juice. Spoon over ingredients in slow cooker. Cover slow cooker and cook for 4 hours on high.

Serves 4 • Preparation 10 minutes plus 12 hours soaking • Cooking 4 hours 10 minutes

Lamb and Eggplant Casserole

1 tablespoon olive oil
1 small eggplant, sliced
8 oz/250g ground lamb
3 large ripe tomatoes, peeled and sliced
salt and freshly ground black pepper
6 fresh basil leaves, finely shredded
4 oz/120g Swiss cheese, grated

1 Heat the oil in a large frying pan over medium heat. Add eggplant and cook until golden brown. Drain on paper towels.

2 Add lamb and cook for 3–4 minutes or until browned. Drain off any excess fat.

3 In a small casserole dish that fits into your slow cooker, arrange a layer of eggplant slices, a layer of lamb and a layer of sliced tomato, and sprinkle with salt and pepper and half of the basil. Cover with grated cheese. Repeat layers until casserole dish is filled, ending with a cheese layer.

4 Place casserole in slow cooker and cook on high for approximately 2 hours. Broil for 1–2 minutes until cheese is browned and bubbly before serving.

Serves 4 • Preparation 35 minutes • Cooking 2 hours

Greek Lamb with Rosemary

3 lb/1½kg lamb stew meat, cubed
1 large white onion, finely sliced
2 teaspoons dried rosemary
¼ teaspoon freshly ground black pepper
¼ teaspoon salt
1 cup chicken stock
¼ cup dry white wine
1 tablespoon all-purpose flour
3 rosemary sprigs

1 Place lamb in slow cooker with all other ingredients except rosemary sprigs.
   Cook on low for approximately 6–8 hours or on high for approximately 5–6 hours.

2 If a thicker gravy is preferred, mix together some of the cooking liquid with all-
   purpose flour. Either pour mixture back into slow cooker and cook on high until
   thickened, stirring occasionally, or gently heat flour mixture on the stovetop in a
   small saucepan, whisking until thickened, before pouring back into the slow cooker.

3 Garnish with rosemary sprigs and serve.

Serves 6 • Preparation 25 minutes • Cooking 5–8 hours

Braised Lamb Shanks

6 lamb shanks
2 medium onions, chopped
2 cloves garlic, crushed
¼ cup all-purpose flour
¼ cup fresh fresh cilantro, chopped
¼ cup beef stock
¾ cup red wine
2 tablespoons tomato paste
juice and zest of 1 orange
3 large sprigs fresh rosemary, leaves removed and chopped

1 Trim excess fat from the lamb shanks.
2 Place the onions and garlic in a slow cooker bowl. Put flour in a plastic bag with the lamb shanks, shake to completely coat the shanks and then place shanks in the cooker on top of the onions and garlic. Sprinkle any leftover flour over the top.
3 Combine all other ingredients in a small bowl and mix thoroughly, then spoon this over the shanks in the cooker.
4 Place lid on and cook on high for 4–5 hours or on low for 9–10 hours. Serve with green beans and mashed potatoes.

Serves 6 • Preparation 20 minutes • Cooking 4–10 hours

Slow Cooked Lamb Roast

3 lb/1½kg lamb roast
2 cloves garlic, cut into slivers
2 sprigs fresh rosemary
2 tablespoons olive oil
1 oz/30g butter
1 large onion, sliced
14 oz/400g canned butter beans, drained and rinsed
¼ cup flat-leaf parsley, chopped
½ cup chicken stock
salt and freshly ground black pepper

1 Make small incisions all over lamb with a very sharp knife, then stuff each with a sliver of garlic and a sprig of rosemary.

2 Heat oil in a large frying pan, cook lamb until browned all over. Remove from pan and transfer to slow cooker.

3 In the same pan, add butter and cook onion for 1–2 minutes or until transparent, then place in slow cooker with remaining ingredients except seasoning.

4 Cover and cook on high for 3–4 hours, or on low for 6–8 hours. Season with salt and pepper.

5 Remove meat from slow cooker and rest for 10 minutes before carving. Serve slices of lamb with beans and parsley sauce.

Serves 4 • Preparation 25 minutes • Cooking 3–8 hours

Pleasing Poultry

Chicken cooked in a slow cooker is a tender, succulent treat. Since overcooked poultry tends to be dry, you will need to watch it little more carefully, and test it from time to time. You'll love how juicy and tender the white meat tastes, compared to standard cooking methods, and you'll get to enjoy lots of rich, flavorful gravies from the slow cooking process.

Drunken Chicken Stew

1 whole chicken, cut into pieces
3 slices of bacon, roughly chopped
3 white onions, thickly sliced
3 carrots, thickly sliced
¼ cup parsley, chopped
1 sprig thyme
12 peppercorns
½ clove garlic, crushed
1¼ cups white wine

1 Soak chicken in salted water for 1 hour. Drain well.
2 Cut bacon into large pieces and combine with all other ingredients in slow cooker. Cook on low for 8 hours or overnight. Remove thyme sprig and serve on a bed of cooked rice, garnished with extra parsley.

Serves 4 • Preparation 25 minutes • Cooking 8–10 hours

Mandarin Orange Chicken

3 white onions, sliced
1 clove garlic, crushed
2 carrots, diced
4 large boneless, skinless chicken breasts
salt and seasoned pepper blend
14 oz/400g canned mandarin oranges in syrup
1 tablespoon honey
2 teaspoons Angostura bitters
3½ oz/100g French onion soup mix
zest of ½ orange, julienned

1 Place onion, garlic and carrots in slow cooker. Coat chicken breasts evenly with mixed salt and pepper blend and place on top of vegetables.

2 Strain oranges and reserve syrup. Mix syrup with honey, bitters, soup mix, and pour into slow cooker. Cook on low for 6–8 hours. After 3 hours, add mandarin segments and orange zest.

3 Remove chicken when cooked. If liquid looks too thin, reduce on a high heat or thicken with 2 tablespoons cornstarch. Serve on rice, and garnish with chopped parsley.

Serves 4 • Preparation 35 minutes • Cooking 6–8 hours

Creamy Chicken and Mushrooms

1 lemon
3 lb/1½kg roasting chicken
1 bouquet garni*
3 carrots, thinly sliced
6 onions, thinly sliced
½ cup chicken stock
salt and freshly ground black pepper
pinch of nutmeg
1 tablespoon toasted, slivered almonds
¼ cup parsley, chopped

Cream sauce
1 tablespoon butter
½ cup half and half
6oz/170g button mushrooms, sliced

1 Halve the lemon, squeeze out the juice and brush it all over the chicken. Place lemon halves in the chicken cavity.

2 Lightly grease the slow cooker and add the bouquet garni. Place the chicken on top and arrange the carrot and onion around the outside. Pour around the stock, season to taste, add nutmeg, then cook for approximately 6 hours on low or 4–5 hours on high (cooking time will vary depending on the tenderness of the chicken).

3 To make the sauce, heat butter in large skillet. Add mushrooms and sauté until golden. Remove about ½ cup of chicken stock from slow cooker and add to mushrooms. Bring to a boil. Stir in cream, reduce heat to simmer and let mixture reduce and thicken. Pour over chicken to serve.

*Bouquet garni is a collection of herbs, traditionally fresh parsley, fresh or dried thyme, and bay leaf that are tied together in a bundle so they can be removed easily at the end of the cooking.

Serves 4–5 • Preparation 40 minutes • Cooking 4–6 hours

Stuffed Chicken Breasts

200g/7 oz fresh ricotta cheese
1 cup chopped arugula
¼ cup toasted pine nuts
100g/3½ oz roasted red pepper, chopped
salt and freshly ground black pepper
4 chicken breasts, skin on; each 170g/6 oz
2 tablespoons butter
1 cup chicken stock

1 Combine the ricotta, arugula, pine nuts, bell pepper and salt and pepper in a small bowl and mix together until smooth.
2 Place 1–2 tablespoons of ricotta mixture under the skin of each chicken breast.
3 Place the chicken breasts in a slow cooker set on high, sprinkle with more salt and pepper, place 1 teaspoon of butter on each breast and pour the stock around the chicken. Cook for 2 hours on high. Serve the chicken with juices and a arugula salad.

Serves 4 • Preparation 10 minutes • Cooking 2 hours

Chicken Salad with Ginger and Pineapple

3 lb/1½kg roasting chicken
salt and peppercorns
2 cloves garlic
2 small white onions, sliced into rings
1 oz/30g ginger, grated
1 pineapple, cubed
1 red pepper
2 tablespoons Italian salad dressing
¼ cup fresh parsley, chopped

1 Place the chicken in the slow cooker and cover with cold water. Add the salt, peppercorns, garlic and half the onion and ginger and cook on low for approximately 5 hours or on high for 3 hours (cooking time will vary depending on the tenderness of the chicken – the flesh should not be falling off the bones). Remove chicken from stock and allow to cool. Reserve stock for another use.

2 Shred chicken into bite-size pieces. Toss with remaining onion, ginger, pineapple, red pepper, and salad dressing. Garnish with fresh parsley.

Serves 6 • Preparation 35 minutes • Cooking 3–5 hours

Spanish Chicken with Chorizo

8 chicken drumsticks
2 tablespoons olive oil
1 onion, sliced
2 cloves garlic, crushed
1 red bell pepper, sliced
1 yellow bell pepper, sliced
2 teaspoons paprika
3 tablespoons dry sherry
2 cups canned chopped tomatoes
1 bay leaf
1 strip orange zest
2 Spanish chorizo sausages, sliced
⅓ cup pitted black olives
salt and freshly ground black pepper

1 Place the chicken in a large non-stick skillet and cook without oil for 12 minutes, turning occasionally, until golden. Remove the chicken and set aside. Drain any fat from the skillet and discard.

2 Add the oil to the skillet and cook the onion, garlic and bell peppers for 3 minutes, until softened.

3 Transfer the mixture to a slow cooker set on low, add the chicken and the paprika, sherry, tomatoes, bay leaf and orange zest. Bring to temperature and cook for 5 hours.

4 Add the chorizo and olives and cook for a further 30 minutes, then season.

Packed with Mediterranean flavors, this casserole is equally good with rice or crusty bread. You can use stock or orange juice instead of the sherry.

Serves 4 • Preparation 15 minutes • Cooking 5 hours 45 minutes

Moroccan Style Chicken Wings

2 tablespoons vegetable oil
2 lb/1kg chicken wings
1 large onion, finely chopped
1 clove garlic, crushed
¾ in/2cm in piece ginger, grated
½ teaspoon ground turmeric
½ teaspoon ground cumin
1 cinnamon stick
¼ cup cider vinegar
2 cups apricot nectar
salt and freshly ground black pepper
3 oz/90g pitted prunes
3 oz/90g dried apricots
1 tablespoon honey
¼ cup lemon juice

1 Heat the oil in a large saucepan and brown the chicken wings in batches. Remove browned wings to a plate. Add the onion to the pan and cook for 2 minutes. Stir in the garlic and cook for an additional minute.

2 Transfer the onion and garlic to the slow cooker. Add the chicken, ginger and spices, and stir to coat wings with spices. Add the vinegar and apricot nectar, season to taste and cook on low for 6 hours.

3 Add the prunes, apricots, honey and lemon juice to the cooker and simmer for 2 more hours. Remove lid, turn to high and simmer for 35 minutes. If a thicker sauce is desired, remove the wings and fruit to a serving platter and simmer until the sauce reduces and thickens. Serve wings immediately on a bed of steamed couscous and pour over the sauce. Garnish with parsley.

Serves 6 • Preparation 40 minutes • Cooking 9 hours

Chicken Crêpes

3 lb/1½kg roasting chicken
2 chicken bouillon cubes, crumbled
1 onion, chopped
3 sprigs parsley
1 sprig thyme
4 oz/120g butter
1 spring onion, finely chopped
21 oz/600g button mushrooms, sliced
4 tablespoons all-purpose flour
salt and freshly ground black pepper
1½ cups milk
1 tablespoon dry sherry

2 tablespoons heavy cream
3 hard-boiled eggs, chopped

Crêpe batter
2 cups all-purpose flour
pinch of salt
2 eggs, beaten
1 tablespoon olive oil
2 cups milk

1 Place chicken in slow cooker, add bouillon cubes, onion and herbs and cover with water. Cook on low for 4–5 hours or high for 3–4 hours. Remove chicken and chop flesh finely, discarding skin and bones. Reserve ½ cup stock. Melt butter in frying pan and sauté green onions and mushrooms until softened but not brown. Blend in flour, season and cook for 1 minute.

2 Combine the milk and reserved stock and add to the pan gradually, stirring. Add sherry and cream, then cook gently until stock thickens. Adjust seasoning if necessary and fold through cooked chicken and hard-boiled eggs. Keep mixture warm in slow cooker on high, with lid slightly ajar.

3 To make batter, sift the flour and salt together and make a well in the center. Add the eggs, oil, and one cup of milk. Beat gradually drawing in flour from the sides. Slowly add remaining milk and 4 tablespoons water, making a thin batter. Cover and set aside for at least an hour. Heat a little butter in a heavy-based 6 in/15cm frying pan. Add a little batter and tilt pan so that batter spreads evenly. When cooked on one side, turn and cook other side. Pile crêpes in a tea towel and keep warm.

4 Preheat the oven to 360°F/180°C. Place a spoonful of chicken sauce onto each crêpe, roll up and place into a greased ovenproof dish. Spoon over some of the sauce and bake for about 10 minutes. Serve remaining sauce on the side.

Serves 6–8 (about 16 crêpes) • Preparation 50 minutes • Cooking 3–5 hours

Chicken a la King

3lb/1½kg roasting chicken
2 chicken bouillon cubes, crumbled
salt and freshly ground black pepper
1 bouquet garni*
3 white onions, sliced
1 oz/30g butter
2–3 tablespoons all-purpose flour
1¼ cups milk

2 tablespoons dry sherry
2 tablespoons Dijon mustard
1 red bell pepper, finely chopped
12 oz/340g canned mushrooms, drained
4 green onions, chopped
4 puff pastry shells
¼ cup fresh parsley, chopped

1 Place chicken, bouillon cubes, salt and pepper, bouquet garni and onions in slow cooker. Cover with cold water and cook on low for approximately 4–6 hours or on high for 3–4 hours.

2 When chicken is cooked, allow to cool and chop into small pieces. Strain cooking juices, reserving 1¼ cups for the sauce. Keep remaining juices for another use. Preheat oven to temperature on puff pastry package.

3 Heat the butter in a saucepan over low heat, add 1 tablespoon of flour and stir for a minute or two. Combine milk and reserved chicken stock and gradually stir into flour and butter mixture, whisking constantly. Bring to a boil, then reduce heat and add sherry and mustard. Stir until thickened. Gently fold in cubed chicken, bell pepper, mushrooms and green onions.

4 Pour sauce mixture into the empty slow cooker and keep hot on high setting. Bake puff pastry shells according to package directions. To serve, spoon chicken mixture into shells and garnish with fresh parsley

*Bouquet garni is a collection of herbs, traditionally fresh parsley, fresh or dried thyme, and bay leaf that are tied together in a bundle so they can be removed easily at the end of the cooking.

Serves 4 • Preparation 40 minutes • Cooking 3–6 hours

Favorite Fish and Seafood

To most people, the methods of cooking fish are limited to frying and baking – it is not generally considered as the basis for a meal cooked in a slow cooker. In actual fact, fish, with its delicate flesh, cooks beautifully in the slow cooker and tastes superb. Tender and juicy, it also retains its shape and texture well, providing it is not overcooked. Do remember that fish will not take as long to cook as other foods, so lift the lid from time to time towards the end of the cooking period and check the tenderness of the flesh.

Citrus and Tarragon Fish

21 oz/600g white fish fillets (such as whitefish, tilapia, sole, flounder)
salt and freshly ground black pepper
8 large sprigs tarragon
2 oranges, each cut into four slices
2 lemons, each cut into four slices
4 tablespoons dry white wine

1 Cut four pieces of aluminium foil and lightly butter each. Place a piece of fish on
   each foil sheet and season to taste.

2 Lay a tarragon sprig on each piece of fish then a slice of orange and a slice of lemon
   side by side. Turn up the sides of the foil and spoon 1 tablespoon wine over each
   fish piece, then fold over the foil and seal the packets. Place in the slow cooker and
   cook on high for 1–1½ hours or on low for 2–2½ hours.

3 To serve, place parcels on serving places, open the top of each packet and replace
   the cooked herb sprigs and citrus slices with fresh herb sprigs and citrus slices.
   Alternatively, carefully transfer the fish to the plate, replace the herbs and citrus
   slices, and spoon the juices over the top.

Serves 4 • Preparation 25 minutes • Cooking 1–2½ hours

Slow Cooker Paella

1 tablespoon olive oil
2 onions, chopped
2 cloves garlic, crushed
4 sprigs fresh thyme, leaves removed and stalks discarded
zest of 1 lemon, finely grated
4 ripe tomatoes, chopped
2½ cups short-grain white rice
pinch of saffron threads, soaked in 2 cups water
5 cups chicken or fish stock, warmed
10 oz/290g peas
2 red bell peppers, chopped
2 lb/1kg mussels, scrubbed and debearded
1 lb/500g firm white fish fillets, chopped
10 oz/290g raw shrimp, shelled
8 oz/250g scallops
3 calamari, cleaned and sliced
¼ cup fresh parsley, chopped

1 Preheat slow cooker on high. Add the oil and the onion and stir, then add the garlic, thyme, lemon zest and tomatoes and cook for 15 minutes.

2 Add the rice and saffron mixture and warmed stock. Simmer, stirring occasionally, for 1½ hours or until the rice has absorbed almost all the liquid.

3 Stir in the peas, bell peppers and mussels and cook for 20 minutes. Add the fish, prawns (shrimp) and scallops and cook for 20 minutes. Stir in the calamari and parsley and cook for 20 minutes longer or until the seafood is cooked.

Serves 8 • Preparation 35 minutes • Cooking 60–80 minutes

Tuna Noodle Casserole

14 oz/400g canned corn kernels, drained
¼ red bell pepper, chopped
14 oz/400g canned tuna, drained
4 oz/120g mushrooms, chopped
1 cup half and half
8 oz/250g Cheddar cheese, grated
¼ cup fresh parsley, chopped
8 oz/250g dried macaroni pasta

Topping
1 cup soft breadcrumbs
1½ oz/45g butter, melted
1 oz/30g Parmesan cheese, grated
1 teaspoon dried basil

1 Bring a large pot of salted water to a boil. Add the macaroni and cook for 8 minutes or until just firm in the center (al dente). Drain, set aside and keep warm.

2 Place soup, corn, red bell pepper, tuna, mushrooms, cream, cheese and parsley in slow cooker. Mix together and cook on high for 1 hour or on low for about 2 hours, until vegetables have softened.

3 Preheat the oven to 375°F/190°C. Pour tuna mixture into a greased casserole together with macaroni. Mix thoroughly.

4 To make the breadcrumb topping, mix all ingredients together. Sprinkle topping over casserole and bake for 30 minutes or until top is golden brown.

Serves 6–8 • Preparation 35 minutes • Cooking 1½–2½ hours

Shrimp Creole

1 tablespoon olive oil
1 large onion, diced
1 clove garlic, crushed
1 small green bell pepper, diced
3 stalks celery, diced
1 cup tomato sauce
400g/14 oz canned whole peeled tomatoes
1 teaspoon smoked paprika
1 teaspoon salt
¼ teaspoon black pepper
grated zest of 1 lemon
500g/1 lb raw jumbo shrimp, shelled, deveined (leaving tails intact)

1 Heat the oil in a large skillet. Add the onion and cook over a medium heat for 2 minutes. Add the garlic and cook for a further minute, stirring constantly.

2 Combine onion and garlic and all ingredients, except shrimp, in a slow cooker and cook on high for 2½ hours.

3 Add the shrimp, stir and reduce heat. Continue to cook on low for another hour.

Serves 4 • Preparation 25 minutes • Cooking 3 hours 35 minutes

Cod with Browned Butter Sauce

1 kg/2 lb cod or skatewing
3 teaspoons salt
1 tablespoon white wine vinegar
1 bay leaf
1 onion, sliced
4 whole black peppercorns
4 sprigs parsley, chopped
grated zest of 1 lemon
2 tablespoons chopped fresh dill
1 tablespoon capers

Browned Butter Sauce
4 tablespoons butter
2 tablespoons white wine vinegar

1 Wash the fish and cut into individual portions.
2 Place in a slow cooker and cover with cold water. Add salt, white wine vinegar, bay leaf, onion and peppercorns and cook for 2 hours and 20 minutes on low.
3 Carefully remove the fish from the slow cooker and transfer to a heated serving dish and keep warm while making the sauce. Sprinkle parsley, lemon zest, dill and capers over fish.
4 To make the sauce, heat a small skillet, add the butter and heat carefully until it begins to turn brown, being careful not to burn it. Pour over fish. Add the white wine vinegar to skillet and reduce by half – this only takes a second. Pour over fish as well and serve immediately with lemon wedges.

Serves 6 • Preparation 5 minutes • Cooking 2 hours 30 minutes

Meatless Meals

More and more people are becoming aware of the advantages of a partly or totally vegetarian diet. Whether the reasons are economical or philosophical, there are hundreds of delicious ways to go meatless.

Savory Zucchini Custards

1 oz/30g butter
¼ cup white onion, finely chopped
8 oz/250g zucchini, grated
salt and freshly ground black pepper
2 oz/60g Parmesan cheese, grated
2 oz/60g Cheddar cheese, grated
⅓ cup heavy cream
2 large eggs, beaten

1 Heat butter in a frying pan and sauté onions for 10–15 minutes until tender and just beginning to brown.

2 Tip zucchini into clean absorbent paper and squeeze dry. Increase the heat in the pan, add the zucchini and toss for 5 minutes or so. Cover pan and cook for several minutes longer over low heat, until zucchini is tender. Season to taste and pour into a bowl.

3 Add cheese to the bowl, pour in cream and stir well. Fold eggs into mixture, then taste and adjust seasoning if necessary. (The mixture may be refrigerated at this stage until ready to cook. If you do this, allow a longer cooking time.)

4 Grease 4 small ramekins and pour custard into each. Put dishes into slow cooker, and pour enough water into the base of the cooker to come approximately halfway up the sides of the dishes. Cook on low for 1 hour with lid ajar.

5 Cook, covered, for another 3 hours, testing for firmness at the end of that time.

Test for firmness by inserting a knife blade into one of the custards – the blade should come out clean.

Serves 4 • Preparation 40 minutes • Cooking 4 hours

Spinach Souffles

8 oz/250g cooked spinach, stems removed
4 oz/120g cream cheese
2 small eggs
½ cup milk
1 small onion, peeled and chopped
¼ teaspoon salt
freshly ground black pepper
½ teaspoon dried basil
1 oz/30g Parmesan cheese, grated
8 fresh basil sprigs

1 Drain spinach or silverbeet until as dry as possible, then process in a food processor or blender until finely chopped. Add remaining ingredients and half the basil and blend until very smooth.

2 Pour mixture into 6–8 small, buttered ovenproof dishes and cover each with aluminum foil. Place dishes in the slow cooker and pour enough water into the base of the slow cooker to come approximately halfway up the sides of the dishes. Cover with lid and cook on high for approximately 1½ hours or on low for 2½ hours.

3 To serve, sprinkle with extra grated cheese and garnish with a basil sprig.

This dish makes a delicious light lunch served with a salad and fresh, warm bread.

Serves 6–8 • Preparation 35 minutes • Cooking 1½–2½ hours

Vegetable Casserole

1 lb/500g potatoes, peeled and thickly sliced
1 lb/500g very ripe tomatoes, peeled and sliced
½ teaspoon sugar
2 white onions, thinly sliced
2 green or red bell peppers, thinly sliced
2 lb/1kg small zucchini, sliced
salt and freshly ground black pepper
1 clove garlic, crushed
1 teaspoon dried basil
1 oz/30g butter
1 oz/30g Parmesan cheese, grated
¼ cup parsley, chopped

1 Boil the potatoes until slightly tender. Sprinkle the tomatoes with sugar.
2 Grease the base of the slow cooker and layer in the vegetables, starting with the onion. Sprinkle each layer with salt, pepper, garlic and basil. Finish with a layer of tomatoes, then dot with butter. Pour over any juice from tomato slices.
3 Cook on high for approximately 3 hours or on low for approximately 5 hours. Serve sprinkled with grated cheese and parsley.

Serves 8 • Preparation 35 minutes • Cooking 3–5 hours

Vegetable Tagine

1 tablespoon olive oil
1 onion, chopped
1 teaspoon ground coriander
1 teaspoon ground cumin
1 teaspoon allspice
1 jalapeno pepper, seeded and finely chopped
400g/14 oz canned chopped tomatoes
2 x 400g/14 oz canned chickpeas, rinsed, drained
400g/14 oz butternut squash, diced
2 cups reduced-salt vegetable stock
⅓ cup couscous
½ cup plain yogurt
1 tablespoon chopped fresh Italian parsley to garnish
1 tablespoon chopped fresh mint to garnish

1 Heat the oil in a large skillet. Add the onion and cook over a medium heat for 5 minutes or until the onion softens. Add the spices and pepper and cook for 2 minutes or until fragrant.

2 Transfer to a slow cooker set on high, then stir in the tomatoes, chickpeas, squash and stock and cook for 2 hours.

3 Add the couscous, stir and cover, then turn the cooker off. Let sit for 15 minutes until the couscous is soft.

4 Serve topped with a dollop of yogurt. Sprinkle with parsley and mint.

Serves 6 • Preparation 10 minutes • Cooking 2 hours 25 minutes

Pizza with Slow Cooked Tomato Sauce

Sauce
1½ lb/750g soft ripe tomatoes, peeled
and chopped
2 tablespoons tomato paste
few dashes Angostura bitters
1 small white onion, finely chopped
salt and freshly ground black pepper
1 teaspoon sugar
¼ teaspoon dried garlic
½ teaspoon Italian seasoning

Pizza Dough
1 package active dry yeast
1 teaspoon sugar
1 lb/500g all-purpose flour
pinch of salt
1 tablespoon butter
1 tablespoon vegetable oil

1 Combine all sauce ingredients in slow cooker and allow to cook on low overnight.
   If the mixture is too thin the next morning, turn cooker to high and cook, uncovered,
   until thickened and reduced. Allow to cool.

2 To make the dough, dissolve the yeast into a large bowl. Add sugar and 1¼ cups
   lukewarm water until yeast has dissolved, sprinkle a little of the flour onto surface
   and set aside in a warm place until mixture froths.

3 Sift the flour and salt together and rub in butter. Pour in frothy yeast mixture and
   mix with a wooden spoon, then turn out onto a floured board and knead for at
   least 5 minutes. Shape into a round and set aside in a warm place until dough has
   doubled in size.

4 Preheat the oven to 425°F/220°C. Roll dough out thinly, place on greased pizza tray
   or heated pizza stone and prick surface all over with a fork.

5 Brush pizza with vegetable oil and spread generously with tomato sauce. Add
   preferred pizza toppings (for example, cheeses, olives, basil), then place pizza in
   oven and cook for about 50 minutes.

Serves 6–8 • Preparation 50 minutes • Cooking 8–10 hours

Herbed Cannelloni with Tomato Sauce

8 oz/250g cottage cheese
1 oz/30g Parmesan cheese, grated
1 teaspoon Italian seasoning
6 green onions, finely chopped
salt and freshly ground black pepper
few drops Angostura bitters (optional)
8 instant cannelloni tubes

Tomato Sauce
1 cup canned crushed tomatoes
3–4 green onions, chopped
2 teaspoons Worcestershire sauce
1 large clove garlic, crushed

1 Bring a large saucepan of salted water to a boil, add the pasta tubes and cook for
   8 minutes or until just firm in the center (al dente). Drain, set aside and keep warm.
   Place the cheeses, Italian seasoning, green onions, salt and pepper in a bowl and
   mix thoroughly.

2 To make the sauce, mix together all ingredients.

3 Lightly butter the base of the slow cooker. Spoon cheese mixture into cannelloni
   tubes. Spoon a little tomato sauce into the cooker, then arrange the stuffed cannelloni
   tubes in the cooker and spoon over remainder of sauce. Cook for 1–1½ hours on high
   or 2–2½ hours on low. Serve sprinkled with extra Parmesan cheese and parsley sprigs.

Serves 3–4 • Preparation 25 minutes • Cooking 1½–2½ hours

Mushroom Ragout

2 oz/60g butter
2 lb/1kg mushrooms, sliced
10 green onions, chopped into 25mm/1 in lengths
2 oz/60g French onion soup mix
freshly ground black pepper
1 tablespoon sweet paprika
1–1½ cups sour cream
½ cup fresh parsley, finely chopped

1 Heat butter in a large frying pan, add mushrooms and green onions and sauté for
   approximately 10 minutes. Add onion soup mix, stir through and cook for about
   5 minutes.
2 Mix together pepper, paprika and sour cream and stir into mushroom mixture. Spoon
   mixture into slow cooker and cook on high for approximately 1–1½ hours or on low for
   2–3 hours. Just before serving, stir in chopped parsley. Serve with brown rice.

Serves 4 • Preparation 35 minutes • Cooking 1–3 hours

White Bean Stew

1 tablespoon olive oil
1 onion, finely diced
2 cloves garlic, crushed
1 red bell pepper, diced
1 jalapeño pepper, seeded and diced
1 teaspoon sweet paprika
14 oz/400g canned diced tomatoes
2 cups vegetable stock
8 oz/250g new potatoes, quartered
8 oz/250g sweet potato, diced
1 carrot, sliced
14 oz/400g canned cannellini beans, rinsed and drained
7 oz/200g Savoy cabbage, shredded
¼ cup fresh fresh cilantro, chopped
salt and freshly ground black pepper

1 Heat oil in a large skillet over medium heat. Cook onion, garlic, and peppers until soft. Add paprika and cook for an additional 1–2 minutes.

2 Transfer contents of frying pan to a slow cooker set on high and add tomatoes and vegetable stock. Stir to combine, then add potato, sweet potato and carrot. Bring to a boil. Reduce heat to low, cover, and simmer for 1½ hours until vegetables are tender.

3 Add beans, cabbage, cilantro, and season with salt and pepper. Simmer for an additional 30 minutes, or until cabbage is cooked. Serve with warm, crusty bread.

This dish is delicious with crusty bread.

Serves 4 • Preparation 35 minutes • Cooking 1½–2½ hours

Eggplant and Tomato Casserole

1 medium eggplant, cubed
250g/8 oz tomatoes, sliced
2 cloves garlic, crushed
¼ teaspoon Cayenne pepper or dash of Tabasco
1cm/½ in ginger, grated
1 teaspoon ground coriander
2 bay leaves
1 tablespoon sugar
½ cup plain yogurt

1 Cover eggplant with a handful of salt and allow to stand for approximately an hour. Rinse and drain well.

2 Combine eggplant with all remaining ingredients except yogurt. Spoon into slow cooker and cook on low for approximately 4 hours. Test to see whether eggplant is cooked.

3 Turn setting to high, stir in yogurt and heat through. Remove bay leave and serve. Top each serving with breadcrumbs toasted in butter if desired.

Serves 4 • Preparation 90 minutes • Cooking 4 hours

Vegetable Curry

2 tablespoons vegetable oil
2 lb/1kg leeks, thinly sliced and washed
1 lb/500g baby carrots, scrubbed and sliced diagonally
4 stalks celery, finely chopped
½ clove garlic, crushed
1 tablespoon curry powder
¾ cup vegetable stock
2 teaspoons cornstarch
salt and freshly ground black pepper
6 green onions, sliced diagonally

1 Heat the oil in a frying pan and lightly sauté the leeks, carrots and celery. Spoon vegetables into slow cooker. Add garlic and curry powder to frying pan and cook for 1–2 minutes.

2 Blend stock with cornstarch, add to frying pan and bring to a boil, stirring constantly. Pour mixture into slow cooker and season. Cook on low for approximately 4 hours or on high for approximately 2–3 hours (test for tenderness after this, as cooking time can very greatly according to the tenderness of the vegetables).

3 When vegetables are cooked, add green onions. Serve with rice.

Serves 4–6 • Preparation 30 minutes • Cooking 2–4 hours

Mushroom Barley Risotto

1 tablespoon olive oil
1 onion, diced
250g/½ lb button mushrooms, coarsely chopped
3 large Portobello mushrooms, sliced
¼ cup chopped fresh parsley
1 tablespoon chopped fresh thyme
2 cloves garlic, crushed
¾ cup pearl barley
4 cups vegetable stock
2 tablespoons tomato paste
salt and freshly ground black pepper
¼ cup grated Parmesan cheese

1 Heat oil in a large heavy-based saucepan over medium heat. Add onion and sauté for 4 minutes. Add all mushrooms and sauté until golden brown, about 15 minutes. Add the parsley, thyme, garlic and barley and stir for 1 minute.

2 Transfer to a slow cooker set on high, add 4 cups of stock, cover and cook until liquid is almost absorbed and barley is almost tender, about 3 hours.

3 Stir in tomato paste, check for seasoning and cook for a further hour. Until barley is tender and mixture is creamy.

4 Stir in cheese and season again if necessary.

Serves 4 • Preparation 15 minutes • Cooking 4 hours 20 minutes

Leeks with Beans

8 oz/250g dried black eyed (navy) beans, soaked overnight
1 tablespoon vegetable oil
1 large onion, chopped
2 cloves garlic, crushed
1 lb/500g leeks, sliced and washed
¼ cup fresh parsley, chopped
6 tomatoes, peeled, seeded and chopped
1 tablespoon sugar
1 teaspoon dry mustard
2 bay leaves
½ teaspoon dried marjoram
1 tablespoon tomato paste
¼ cup vegetable stock
salt and freshly ground black pepper

1 Drain the beans well. Heat the oil in a frying pan and sauté the onion and garlic, then add the leeks and sauté until softened. Spoon leek mixture, beans and all remaining ingredients into slow cooker.
2 Cover and cook on low for approximately 8–9 hours or on high for 4–5 hours. Garnish with extra parsley.

Serves 6 • Preparation 25 minutes • Cooking 4–9 hours

Spicy Vegetable Stew

1 tablespoon olive oil
1 onion, finely diced
2 cloves garlic, crushed
1 red bell pepper, diced
1 jalapeño pepper, seeded and diced
1 teaspoon sweet paprika
400g/14 oz canned diced tomatoes
2 cups vegetable stock
250g/½ lb baby potatoes, cut into quarters
300g/10 oz sweet potato, diced
1 carrot, sliced
1 cup fresh peas
400g/14 oz canned cannellini beans, rinsed, drained
3 cups shredded savoy cabbage
2 tablespoons freshly chopped cilantro
salt and freshly ground black pepper

1 Heat oil in a large skillet over medium heat. Cook onion, garlic, bell pepper and jalapeño pepper until soft. Add sweet paprika and cook until aromatic.

2 Transfer contents of the skillet into a slow cooker set on high and add tomatoes and vegetable stock. Stir to combine, then add potato, sweet potato and carrot. Bring to a boil. Reduce heat to low. Cover and simmer for 1½ hours until vegetables are tender.

3 Add peas, beans, cabbage and cilantro and season with salt and pepper. Simmer for a further 30 minutes or until cabbage is cooked.

4 Serve with crusty bread.

Serves 4 • Preparation 25 minutes • Cooking 2 hours 15 minutes

Breads and Desserts

There is nothing like the aroma of fresh baked bread, but let's face it—who has the time? The slow cooker isn't just great for one-dish dinners, it's great for baking, too. Bread is just one of the many wonders that bakes itself. Try the sesame coated Half and Half bread, or the hearty Cracked Wheat Bread. And don't forget about dessert. Slow cookers let you start dessert early in the day and forget about it til dinnertime. Slow cooked desserts are rich and moist, so may have to cook a little extra for second helpings.

Yogurt Banana Bread

2 oz/60g butter
4 oz/120g granulated sugar
1 egg, lightly beaten
2 large, ripe bananas, mashed
8 oz/250g self-raising whole wheat flour
pinch of salt
4 oz/120g walnuts, roughly chopped
3 tablespoons plain yogurt
½ teaspoon ground cinnamon
1½ teaspoons powdered sugar

1 Cream together the butter and granulated sugar. Add egg, mashed bananas and mix thoroughly.
2 Mix flour and salt together and add walnuts. Add flour mixture and yogurt alternately to the banana mixture in small quantities, and blend thoroughly.
3 Pour mixture into greased loaf pan and cover tightly with foil. Place in slow cooker and cover. Cook on high for approximately 2½–3 hours or until a toothpick inserted in the middle comes out clean. Allow to cool for 10 minutes, then let rest on wire rack until fully cooled.
4 Combine cinnamon and sugar and sprinkle over the top of the loaf before serving.

Makes 1 loaf • Preparation 40 minutes • Cooking 3 hours

Cherry Walnut Fruit Cake

8 oz/250g butter
8 oz/250g brown sugar
5 eggs, beaten until frothy
1 lb/500g golden raisins
6 oz/170g maraschino cherries
4 oz/120g walnut pieces
7 oz/200g all-purpose flour
1 tablespoon milk

1 Cream the butter and sugar in a bowl. Add eggs gradually. Fold in fruit, walnuts and flour, then add milk.

2 Grease a 9" springform cake pan and line the bottom and sides with parchment paper. Spoon in the cake batter and cover tightly with foil. Place in slow cooker and cover. Cook on high setting for 4½–5 hours, taking care not to remove the foil or the slow cooker lid until the last hour of cooking.

Makes 1 cake • Preparation 30 minutes • Cooking 5 hours

Mixed Berry Cake

4 oz/120g butter
¼ cup sugar
1½ teaspoon vanilla extract
2 eggs, lightly beaten
2 cups all-purpose flour
2 teaspoons baking powder
salt
1 teaspoon pumpkin pie spice
½ cup milk
¾ cup mixed berries, such as strawberries, blueberries, raspberries, or blackberries
½ teaspoon cinnamon
1½ teaspoons powdered sugar

1 Cream the butter, sugar and vanilla, then fold eggs into mixture.

2 Sift flour, baking powder, and salt together and stir in pumpkin pie spice. Fold ⅓ of flour mixture into the cream, butter and egg mixture. Add half of the milk, then another third of flour mixture, rest of milk and rest of flour mixture, gently folding each time to combine. Spoon into a greased and floured 9" springform pan, and arrange berries on top.

3 Cover tightly with foil and place in slow cooker. Cook on high setting for approximately 3 hours, taking care not to remove the foil or slow cooker lid until the last hour of cooking. Combine cinnamon and sugar. Dust cake with cinnamon sugar before serving. Serve with whipped cream if desired.

Serves 8 • Preparation 30 minutes • Cooking 3 hours

Coffee Cake

4½ oz/130g butter
¾ cup granulated sugar
½ teaspoon vanilla extract
3 eggs
1½ cups all-purpose flour, sifted
1½ teaspoons baking powder
pinch of salt
1 tablespoon milk

Coffee syrup
1 cup strong black coffee
⅓ cup sugar
2 tablespoons brandy or whiskey

1 Beat the butter until softened, then gradually beat in the sugar and vanilla until mixture is light and fluffy. Add eggs one at a time, beating well after each.

2 Sift together flour, baking powder and salt and fold into butter mixture. Add milk. Spoon into a greased 9" springform pan, cover tightly with foil, and place in slow cooker. Cook on high for about 2–2½ hours, taking care not to remove either the foil or the slow cooker lid until the last hour to 30 minutes of cooking time.

3 Remove pan from slow cooker, allow to cool for about 10 minutes, then turn cake out of pan and allow to cool on a wire rack. When cold, replace in pan.

4 To make the coffee syrup, place the coffee into a saucepan, add sugar and ⅔ cup water and heat until sugar dissolves. Add the brandy or whiskey and bring to a boil, stirring occasionally. Boil for 3 minutes. Allow to cool.

5 Pour cold syrup over cake and refrigerate overnight. Serve with whipped cream.

Serves 8 • Preparation 30 minutes • Cooking 2½ hours

Fruit and Nut Bread

½ cup unprocessed bran
¾ cup sugar
½ cup golden raisins
1 cup raisins
1¼ cups buttermilk
1½ cups whole wheat flour
1½ teaspoons baking powder
¼ cup wheatgerm
¼ cup walnuts, chopped

1 Combine bran, sugar, golden raisins, raisins and milk and allow to stand for approximately 15 minutes.
2 Mix together the flour, baking powder, wheatgerm and walnuts, then add to the fruit mixture and mix thoroughly. Spoon mixture into a greased 9" springform pan, smooth the surface and cover with aluminum foil.
3 Place in slow cooker and cook on high for approximately 3 hours, taking care not to remove either the foil or the slow cooker lid until the last hour of cooking. Remove foil and allow loaf to cool slightly, then turn out onto a wire rack to cool completely.
4 Serve sliced, spread with butter and honey or apricot jam.

Makes 1 loaf • Preparation 40 minutes • Cooking 3 hours

Country Bread

1 package active dry yeast
2 teaspoons honey
8 oz/250g all-purpose flour
4 oz/120g whole wheat flour
2 teaspoons baking powder
1 teaspoon salt
½ cup finely ground oats
2 tablespoons/30g butter

1 Blend together yeast and honey and pour in 1¼ cups warm water. Sprinkle a little of the flour onto the surface of the liquid and stand bowl over a slow cooker set on low until mixture froths.

2 Mix together all dry ingredients and rub in the butter. Make a well in the center of the dry ingredients and pour in frothy yeast mixture. Stir with a wooden spoon, then turn out onto a floured board and knead for about 10 minutes. Shape into a round and place back into bowl and set aside on the slow cooker (still set on low) until dough has doubled in size.

3 Punch down risen dough and form into a round. Place in a greased 9" springform pan, cover, and place pan in the slow cooker. Cook on high for about 3–4 hours, then turn loaf out and allow to cool on a wire rack.

Makes 1 loaf • Preparation 30 minutes • Cooking 3–4 hours

Herb Bread

1 package active dry yeast
1 teaspoon sugar
1 lb/500g all-purpose flour
1 teaspoon vegetable or garlic salt
2 teaspoons dried mixed herbs
2 teaspoons dried chives, crumbled
2 sprigs parsley, chopped
2 tablespoons/30g butter

1 Crumble the yeast into a bowl, stir in sugar and 1¼ cups lukewarm water until yeast has dissolved. Sprinkle with a little of the flour and stand in a warm spot until mixture froths.

2 Mix together flour, salt and herbs. Rub in the butter, then make a well in the center of the dry ingredients and pour in frothy yeast mixture. Stir well with a wooden spoon, then turn out onto a floured board and knead for about 5 minutes. Shape into a round, place back into bowl and set aside on a slow cooker set on low until dough has doubled in size.

3 Punch down risen dough and form into a round. Place in a greased 9" springform pan and set aside on the slow cooker again until dough has doubled in size.

4 Cover with aluminum foil and place in the slow cooker and cook on high for 2–3 hours, taking care not to remove either the foil or the slow cooker lid until the last hour of cooking. Turn loaf out and cool on a wire rack.

Makes 1 loaf • Preparation 40 minutes • Cooking 2–3 hours

Cracked Wheat Bread

1½ package active dry yeast
1 tablespoon blackstrap molasses
1 lb/500g whole wheat flour
8 oz/250g all-purpose flour
¾ cup cracked wheat
1 teaspoon salt

1 In a large bowl, blend together yeast and blackstrap molasses, then add 2 cups warm water. Mix well, sprinkle a little flour onto surface and set aside in a slow cooker set on low until mixture froths.

2 Mix together all dry ingredients. Pour in frothy yeast mixture and stir with a wooden spoon, then turn out onto a floured board and knead for at least 5 minutes, until mixture is smooth and pliable. Shape into a rough loaf, place in a greased 12 x 22cm loaf pan and set aside on the slow cooker (still set on low) until dough has doubled in size.

3 Preheat the oven to 400°F/200°C. Bake the bread for 10 minutes, then reduce temperature to 375°F/190°C. Continue baking for about another 40 minutes, then test loaf – when cooked, loaf will give a hollow sound when rapped with knuckles. Turn loaf out of pan and allow to cool on a wire rack.

Makes 1 loaf • Preparation 90 minutes • Cooking 2 hours

Half and Half Bread

1 package active dry yeast
2 teaspoons honey
2⅓ cups warm milk
1 lb/500g all-purpose flour
1 lb/500g whole wheat flour
1 tablespoon baking powder
1 tablespoon salt
2 oz/60g butter
6 tablespoons sesame seeds
1 egg white

1 Blend together yeast and honey, then add the milk. Sprinkle a little of the flour on top of the liquid. Stand bowl in a warm spot until mixture froths.

2 Mix together the flours, baking powder and salt. Rub in the butter. Make a well in center of the dry ingredients and pour in the frothy yeast mixture. Stir well with a wooden spoon, then turn out onto a floured board and knead for about 5 minutes. Shape into a round, place back into bowl and set aside on a slow cooker set on low until dough has doubled in size.

3 Grease two 1 lb/500g loaf pans and sprinkle half the sesame seeds around bottom and sides of each pan. Punch down risen dough and form into two rough loaves, then place in pans. Set aside on the slow cooker again until dough has risen to the top of the pans.

4 Preheat the oven to 400°F/200°C. Brush risen loaves with egg white and sprinkle with sesame seeds, then place into oven on middle shelf. Bake for 10 minutes, then reduce temperature to 350°F/175°C and bake for an additional 40–45 minutes. Turn loaves out of pans and allow to cool on a wire rack.

Makes 2 loaves • Preparation 90 minutes • Cooking 2 hours

Apricot Mousse

8 oz/250g dried apricots
2 granny smith apples, peeled and thinly sliced
juice and zest of 1 lemon
¼ cup sugar
3 egg whites
½ cup heavy cream, whipped

1 Soak dried apricots in warm water for about 1 hour, then drain well. Place into slow cooker with apples, lemon juice and zest and sugar. Cook on low for 3–4 hours or on high for 2–3 hours, until apricots are soft and apples cooked. Drain fruit, discarding liquid, and purée in a blender or food processor. Chill.

2 Beat egg whites until stiff. Beat the cream in a separate bowl, then fold half the cream into the egg whites. Carefully fold egg white mixture and remaining cream through the fruit purée. Chill. Serve mousse with extra cream and a little grated orange zest.

Serves 4 • Preparation 90 minutes • Cooking 2–4 hours

Ginger Custard with Chocolate Sauce

2 large eggs
1¼ cups milk
1 tablespoon sugar
1 tablespoon crystallized ginger, finely chopped
½ teaspoon ground ginger
¼ teaspoon ground cinnamon

Chocolate sauce
1 oz/30g dark chocolate, grated
2 teaspoons sugar
⅔ cup evaporated milk
2 teaspoons cornstarch

1 To make the sauce, combine the grated chocolate, sugar and half the milk in a small saucepan. Heat gently until chocolate melts, stirring constantly.

2 Mix the cornstarch into the remaining milk, then add to the chocolate mixture and whisk until sauce boils. Reduce heat and simmer for approximately 3 minutes.

3 To make the custard, beat together eggs, milk and sugar, then stir in chopped ginger. Pour into 2–3 small ovenproof dishes. Sprinkle each dish with a little ginger and cinnamon, then cover with aluminium foil, place in slow cooker and cook for approximately 1½ hours on high or 2–2½ hours on low. Serve custards drizzled with hot chocolate sauce.

Serves 2–3 • Preparation 35 minutes • Cooking 1½–2½ hours

Grand Marnier Crème Caramel

6 tablespoons sugar
3 eggs
2½ cups milk
2 tablespoons Grand Marnier

1 Melt half the sugar slowly in a heavy saucepan. Do not stir, just allow to melt into caramel.

2 Butter 4 small heatproof crème caramel molds, then pour the melted sugar quickly into base of dishes and swirl around the sides as high as possible.

3 Beat eggs well and whisk into milk with Grand Marnier and the remaining sugar. Keep whisking until sugar has dissolved, then pour mixture into caramel molds and cover with foil. Place molds into slow cooker and pour sufficient cold water around the bases to come halfway up the sides. Cook on low for approximately 3–4 hours.

4 Remove crème caramels from slow cooker and chill thoroughly. Serve either in the molds or very carefully turned out onto plates, with any caramel left behind spooned over the top.

Serves 4 • Preparation 40 minutes • Cooking 3–4 hours

Butterscotch and Apricot Parfait

1 lb/500g fresh apricots
1 tablespoon sugar
1 cinnamon stick
pinch of ground nutmeg
1–2 ripe mangos, peeled and sliced
½ cup heavy cream, whipped
4 sprigs mint

Butterscotch custard

4 egg yolks
14 oz/400g canned evaporated skim milk
1 teaspoon vanilla extract
1 heaping tablespoon brown sugar

1 To make the custard, beat together all the ingredients until sugar has dissolved, then pour into a greased heatproof basin. Cover basin tightly with foil, place in slow cooker, and pour enough water into cooker to come halfway up the sides of the basin. Cook on low for 3–4 hours. Remove basin from slow cooker, loosen around the rim of the basin with a knife and slip custard onto a warmed plate.

2 Wash apricots and remove pits. Place in the slow cooker with sugar, cinnamon stick, nutmeg, and 1 tablespoon water to prevent sticking. Cook on high for at least 2 hours, until tender and almost mushy. Remove cinnamon stick and drain fruit.

3 Set aside 4–6 mango slices for garnish, then layer apricots, butterscotch custard and mangos in tall parfait glasses until full. Top each glass with a swirl of whipped cream.

Serves 4–6 • Preparation 40 minutes • Cooking 5–6 hours

Ripe Fruit Compote

6 apricots, halved and pitted
5 oz/150g cherries
6 fresh plums
1 apple, sliced
½ cup sugar
rind of 1 orange
3 cloves

1 Combine all ingredients in the slow cooker and cook on low for 2–3 hours or on high for 1–1½ hours. Remove cloves and orange rind and test for sweetness, adding sugar or honey to taste.

2 Allow to cool, then serve with whipped cream.

This is a marvelous recipe for using up overripe fruit.

Serves 4 • Preparation 10 minutes • Cooking 1–3 hours

Cherries Grand Marnier

44 oz/1¼kg canned cherries
rind of 1 orange
2 cinnamon sticks
4 tablespoons Grand Marnier

1 Drain cherries and retain half the syrup. Pour cherries, retained syrup, orange rind and cinnamon sticks into the slow cooker and cook on low for approximately 1 hour. Add half the Grand Marnier and heat through. Remove the cinnamon and orange rind.

2 Serve in individual bowls topped with a scoop of ice cream, a spoonful of the remaining Grand Marnier and a sprinkle of grated chocolate.

Alternatively, for a dinner party, serve the cherries in a large bowl and pour heated flaming Grand Marnier over the cherries at the table.

Serves 8 • Preparation 15 minutes • Cooking 1 hour

Spiced Peaches

handful of cloves
21 oz/600g canned peach halves, with juice
1 cinnamon stick
2 tablespoons brandy, orange liqueur or orange juice

1 Press 5 cloves into each peach half and arrange halves in the base of the slow cooker.
2 Combine peach juice and brandy, liqueur or orange juice, add the cinnamon stick and pour mixture over peaches. Cook on low for 2–3 hours or on high for 1–1½ hours. Serve hot or chilled, with whipped cream.

The peaches will keep in the refrigerator for at least a week.

Serves 4 • Preparation 10 minutes • Cooking 1–3 hours

Bananas with Rum and Honey

6 firm bananas, peeled
2 tablespoons dark rum
1 tablespoon honey
2 tablespoons orange juice
juice of ½ lemon
½ teaspoon ground cinnamon

1 Arrange bananas in base of slow cooker. Combine rum, honey, juices and cinnamon and spoon over and around bananas. Cook on high for approximately ½–¾ hour or on low for approximately 1 hour, until bananas are just tender and syrup is heated through.
2 Serve bananas with scoops of ice cream, with syrup spooned over.

Serves 4–6 • Preparation 15 minutes • Cooking 30–60 minutes

Cherry Compote

1 lb/500g cherries
1½ cups rosé wine
3 tablespoons sugar
1 cinnamon stick
2 tablespoons brandy or Grand Marnier
zest of 1 orange, grated
8 oz/250g strawberries

1 Place cherries in slow cooker, pour over the rosé and add the sugar, cinnamon stick and liqueur. Cover tightly and cook for approximately 2 hours on low.
2 Add the orange zest and strawberries and chill well. Serve with cream.

Serves 6–8 • Preparation 10 minutes • Cooking 2 hours

Mixed Fruit Pudding

6 tablespoons/90g butter
1 cup sugar
2 cups all-purpose flour
1½ teaspoons baking powder
½ teaspoon pumpkin-pie spice
½ teaspoon baking soda
salt
½ cup milk
1 egg
1 tablespoon raisins
1 tablespoon golden raisins
1 tablespoon dried dates, chopped
1 tablespoon dried apricots, chopped
1 tablespoon walnuts, chopped

1 Grease a medium sized baking dish with a little of the butter. In a large bowl, cream the remainder of the butter with sugar until light and soft.

2 Stir flour and baking powder together with pumpkin-pie spice, baking soda and salt to taste. Beat milk and egg together. Stir small quantities of sifted flour and beaten milk alternately into creamed butter mixture. Fold together lightly.

3 Stir in dried fruits and walnuts, and spoon mixture into the baking dish. Cover tightly with foil and tie with kitchen string, forming a loop at the top so that the basin may be easily removed from the slow cooker.

4 Place baking dish in slow cooker and pour enough boiling water around the base to come halfway up the sides. Cook on high for approximately 5 hours. Turn out pudding onto heated serving platter and serve with hot custard.

Serves 6–8 • Preparation 45 minutes • Cooking 5 hours

Creamy Rice Pudding

zest of 1 orange, grated
2½ cups cooked rice
1 cup evaporated milk or 1 cup ordinary milk plus 1 beaten egg
⅔ cup sugar
4 tablespoons/60g butter, softened
½ teaspoon vanilla extract
½ teaspoon ground cinnamon or nutmeg
⅓ cup golden raisins

1 Reserve a little orange zest to garnish, then mix the rice with all other
   ingredients. Lightly grease the slow cooker interior and spoon in
   pudding mixture.
2 Cook on high for approximately 1–2 hours or on low for 4–6 hours.
   Stir occasionally during first hour of cooking. Serve with a little cream
   and a pinch of grated orange zest.

Serves 6 • Preparation 30 minutes • Cooking 1–6 hours

Bread Pudding

4 thin slices stale white bread, buttered
½ cup mixed raisins, golden raisins and currants
3 tablespoons sugar
½ teaspoon grated nutmeg or cinnamon
2 eggs
2½ cups milk
1 teaspoon vanilla extract
zest of ½ orange, grated

1 Remove crusts from bread and cut into thick fingers. Grease an ovenproof dish and arrange bread in layers, buttered-side up. Sprinkle layers with dried fruit, sugar and spice.

2 Beat together eggs, milk and vanilla and stir in orange zest. Pour mixture over layered bread and allow to stand for approximately 30 minutes. Cover dish with lid or foil.

3 Pour 1 cup hot water into the slow cooker, then insert the pudding dish and cook on high for 3–4 hours.

Serves 6 • Preparation 45 minutes • Cooking 3–4 hours

Steamed Orange Cake

2 oranges, peeled and thickly sliced, plus zest of 1 orange
3 oz/90g butter
½ cup sugar
1½ cups self-rising flour
salt
½ cup milk
1 egg, beaten
2 tablespoons honey

1 Grease a medium-sized baking dish that will fit inside slow cooker and arrange orange slices around the base and sides.

2 Cream together butter and sugar until light and fluffy. Stir in flour and salt to taste alternately with milk and egg, then beat until smooth. Stir in grated orange zest.

3 Warm honey and spoon over the base and sides of the orange lined baking dish. Spoon in batter and cover dish with foil and tie with string, forming a loop at the top so that the basin may be easily removed from the slow cooker.

4 Place the baking dish in the slow cooker. Boil 2–4 cups water and pour into base of cooker, and cook on high for approximately 5 hours. Carefully remove the dish and turn out the steamed cake. Slice the cake and serve with a little extra warmed honey and whipped cream, if desired.

Serves 6–8 • Preparation 75 minutes • Cooking 5 hours

Hot Caramel Meringue

¼ cup sugar
1½ cups evaporated milk
1 teaspoon vanilla extract
3 thick slices bread, crusts removed, cubed
⅓ cup golden raisins
⅓ cup raisins, chopped
zest of 1 orange, grated
3 eggs, separated
¼ cup half and half
1 teaspoon lemon juice
⅓ cup sugar
1 teaspoon dried coconut

1 Place sugar in a heavy-based saucepan and heat over low temperature, stirring gently until sugar has dissolved. Once melted, increase heat and allow to cook without stirring until a deep golden brown. Remove from heat.

2 Meanwhile, bring the milk to a boil. Pour boiling milk into the melted sugar gradually, stirring or whisking constantly to form a smooth caramel. Add vanilla.

3 Mix together bread cubes, dried fruits and orange zest. Add caramel and allow to stand for about half an hour.

4 Beat egg yolks and cream, and add lemon juice. Stir gently into cooling caramel mixture. Allow to become cold, then pour into an ovenproof baking dish, cover with foil and tie firmly with kitchen string. Fill the slow cooker with about 2 in/5cm of water and put in the baking dish. Cook on low for 2½–3 hours. Remove dish, take off foil covering and allow to cool.

5 Preheat the oven to 400°F/200°C. Whip the egg whites, gradually adding the sugar, then swirl meringue onto top of cooled pudding and sprinkle with coconut. Place in oven and cook for 15–20 minutes or until meringue is golden brown and crisp.

Serves 4–6 • Preparation 50 minutes • Cooking 2½–3½ hours

Index